Snowy Owls
of the Tundra

By Riley Lawrence

Published in 2018 by
KidHaven Publishing, an Imprint of Greenhaven Publishing, LLC
353 3rd Avenue
Suite 255
New York, NY 10010

Designer: Deanna Paternostro
Editor: Vanessa Oswald

Photo credits: Cover, pp. 9, 13, 15 FotoRequest/Shutterstock.com; back cover, p. 21 (top) Mario7/ Shutterstock.com; p. 5 Erick Margarita Images/Shutterstock.com; p. 7 Robert L Kothenbeutel/ Shutterstock.com; p. 11 Steve Whiston/Shutterstock.com; p. 17 Richard Fitzer/Shutterstock.com; p. 19 Michael C. Gray/Shutterstock.com; p. 21 (bottom) Shakarrigrafie/Shutterstock.com.

Cataloging-in-Publication Data

Names: Lawrence, Riley.
Title: Snowy owls / Riley Lawrence.
Description: New York : KidHaven Publishing, 2018. | Series: Animals of the tundra| Includes index.
Identifiers: ISBN 9781534522282 (pbk.) | 9781534522268 (library bound) | ISBN 9781534522169 (6 pack) | ISBN 9781534522213 (ebook)
Subjects: LCSH: Snowy owl–Juvenile literature.
Classification: LCC QL696.S8 L39 2018 | DDC 598.9'7–dc23

Printed in the United States of America

CPSIA compliance information: Batch #BS17KL: For further information contact Greenhaven Publishing LLC, New York, New York at 1-844-317-7404.

Please visit our website, www.greenhavenpublishing.com. For a free color catalog of all our high-quality books, call toll free 1-844-317-7404 or fax 1-844-317-7405.

Contents

Flying in the Tundra

Snowy owls are as white as snow, which is how they got their name. They live near the Arctic Ocean in the tundra, which is a flat, treeless place with frozen ground and cold weather.

Snowy owls have
bright yellow eyes!

5

Snowy owls are only white at certain times of their lives. When owls are born, they have brown feathers. As males get older, they get whiter. Females have more brown spots than males and are never all white.

male

female

Snowy owls are the largest bird **species** in the Arctic.

A snowy owl has many feathers covering much of its body, including its beak, wings, legs, and feet. These feathers help the owl store heat to stay warm while flying through the chilly winds of the tundra.

Snowy owls can turn their head three-quarters of the way around.

Winged Hunters

Snowy owls have great senses of sight and hearing, which they use while hunting their **prey**. Owls watch from the ground or on a **perch**, such as a tree branch, before swooping down to catch food using their **talons**.

Snowy owls use their strong sense of hearing when listening for animals hiding under snow and plants.

11

When snowy owls have trouble finding food in the tundra, they fly south. They are **carnivores** and are known to eat small animals such as lemmings, mice, rabbits, birds, and fish. In just one year, a snowy owl can eat more than 1,600 lemmings!

In the spring, snowy owls
also steal eggs from birds
such as geese and swans.
They have to be quick!

13

Most owls are nocturnal, which means they are active and hunt at night. However, snowy owls are mainly diurnal. They are active and hunt mostly during the day, but sometimes they hunt at night, too.

A snowy owl can fly at the speed of 50 miles (80 km) per hour.

15

Owl Families

Snowy owls that **mate** are called **breeding pairs**. The males will get the attention of the females by hooting, bowing their body, and lifting their tail. Before breeding can take place, the male searches out a place for the female to build its nest.

When a male snowy owl defends itself from another male owl, it will lower its head and stick it forward. It will also stretch out its wings and raise the feathers on its neck to make it look bigger.

17

A mother snowy owl lays 3 to 11 eggs at a time in its nest. If there is not enough food, the snowy owl may decide not to lay eggs. Breeding generally happens between May and September.

A snowy owl's nest is on the ground.

19

Baby snowy owls hatch about a month after the eggs are laid by the mother snowy owl. Both snowy owl parents **protect** their babies. The father finds and brings food to the babies, and the mother feeds it to them.

Learning More

How tall are snowy owls?	up to 28 inches (71 cm)
What is the wingspan of a snowy owl?	up to 4.8 feet (1.5 m)
How much do snowy owls weigh?	up to 6.5 pounds (3 kg)
How long do snowy owls live?	about 10 years in the wild
What do snowy owls eat?	small animals such as lemmings, mice, rabbits, birds, and fish

Baby Snowy owls, such as this one, grow into cool winged creatures!

Glossary

breeding pair: Two animals (a male and female) that get together to make babies.

carnivore: An animal that eats only meat.

mate: To come together to make babies.

perch: Something a bird sits on.

prey: An animal hunted by other animals for food.

protect: To keep safe.

species: A group of plants or animals that are all the same kind.

talon: A claw, especially one belonging to a bird of prey.

For More Information

Websites

National Geographic Kids

kids.nationalgeographic.com/animals/snowy-owl/#snowy-owl-closeup.jpg

This website provides interesting information about snowy owls for young readers.

National Wildlife Federation

www.nwf.org/Kids/Ranger-Rick/Animals/Birds/Snowy-Owls.aspx

This website includes fun facts about snowy owls and pictures of them in action.

Books

Ehrgott, Jessica, Melissa Hill, and Gail Saunders-Smith. *Snowy Owls*. North Mankato, MN: Capstone Press, 2016.

Murray, Julie. *Snowy Owls*. Minneapolis, MN: ABDO Publishing Company, 2014.

Index